D0518401

WITHDRAWN

The 1980s

Stephen Feinstein

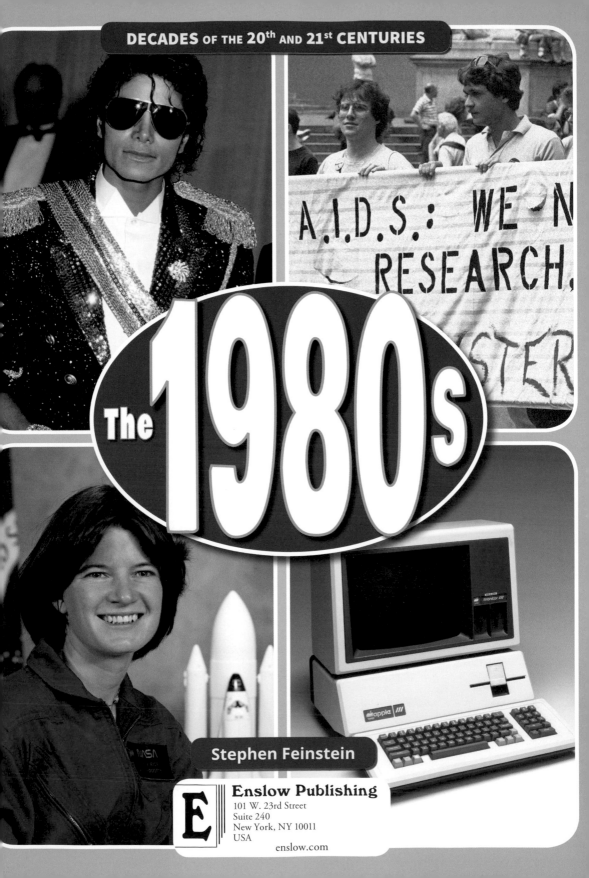

DECADES OF THE 20th AND 21st CENTURIES

The 1980s

A.I.D.S.: WE N
RESEARCH,
STER

Stephen Feinstein

E Enslow Publishing

101 W. 23rd Street
Suite 240
New York, NY 10011
USA

enslow.com

Published in 2016 by Enslow Publishing, LLC.
101 W. 23rd Street, Suite 240, New York, NY 10011

Copyright © 2016 by Enslow Publishing, LLC.
All rights reserved.

No part of this book may be reproduced by any means without the written permission of the publisher.

Library of Congress Cataloging-in-Publication Data

Feinstein, Stephen.
  The 1980s / Stephen Feinstein.
      pages cm. — (Decades of the 20th and 21st centuries)
  Includes bibliographical references and index.
  Summary: "Discusses the decade 1980-1989 in the United States in terms of culture, art, science, and politics"—Provided by publisher.
  Audience: Grade 9 to 12.
  ISBN 978-0-7660-6935-0
  1. United States—Civilization—1945-—Juvenile literature. 2. United States—Politics and government—1981-1989—Juvenile literature. 3. Nineteen eighties—Juvenile literature. I. Title.
  E169.12.F4475 2015
  973.927—dc23

                                   2015010950

Printed in the United States of America

To Our Readers: We have done our best to make sure all Web sites in this book were active and appropriate when we went to press. However, the author and the publisher have no control over and assume no liability for the material available on those Web sites or on any Web sites they may link to. Any comments or suggestions can be sent by e-mail to customerservice@enslow.com.

Photo Credits: ABC Television/Fotos International/Getty Images, p. 35; Andy Hayt/Sports Illustrated/Getty Images, p. 39; Apic/Getty Images/Getty Images, p. 76; © AP Images, pp. 3 (top right), 75; Bill Pierce/The LIFE Images Collection/Getty Images, p. 66; Bob Thomas/Bob Thomas Sports Photography/Getty Images, p. 40; CARLOS GUARDIA/AFP/Getty Images, p. 70; Cynthia Johnson/The LIFE Images Collection/Getty Images, p. 55; Dan Mccoy/The LIFE Images Collection/Getty Images, pp. 18, 87 (top); David Hume Kennerly/3rd Party - Misc/Getty Images, p. 46; Education Images/UIG via Getty Images, p. 14; Erik Hill/Anchorage Daily News/MCT via Getty Images, p. 83; Focus on Sport/Focus on Sport/Getty Images, p. 36; Gordon Gahan/National Geographic/Getty Images, pp. 10, 88 (top); Harry Langdon/Archive Photos/Getty Images, p. 45; Julian Wasser/Hulton Archive/Getty Image, pp. 17, 85, 88 (bottom); Karl Schumacher/The LIFE Images Collection/Getty Images, p. 57; Keystone-France/Gamma-Keystone via Getty Images, pp. 41, 49, 65; Linda Vartoogian/Archive Photos/Getty Images, p. 25; Mark Weiss/WireImage/Getty Images, pp. 22, 87 (bottom); Michael Ochs Archives/Michael Ochs Archives/Getty Images, p. 27; Mike Cameron/Redferns/Getty Images, p. 28; MPI/Archive Photos/Getty Images, p. 50; NASA photo, p. 3 (bottom left); Paramount Pictures/Moviepix/Getty Images, p. 32; Peter Bischoff/PB Archive/Getty Images, p. 21; Peter Charlesworth/LightRocket via Getty Images, pp. 62, 89 (bottom); Ron Galella/WireImage/Ron Galella Collection/Getty Images, pp. 3 (top left), 12, 89 (top); Ron Sachs/Consolidated News Pictures/Getty Images, p. 58; Science & Society Picture Library/SSPL/Getty Images, pp. 3 (bottom right); 73, 78; SHONE/GAMMA/Gamma-Rapho via Getty Images, p. 81; Sovfoto/UIG via Getty Images, p. 61; Terry Smith/The LIFE Images Collection/Getty Images, p. 69; Tony Duffy/Getty Images Sport/Getty Images, p. 42; Vinnie Zuffante/Michael Ochs Archives/Getty Images, p. 31; Visions of America/UIG via Getty Images, p. 53; White House Photos/Hulton Archive/Getty Images, p. 8; William Foley/The LIFE Images Collection/Getty Images, p. 54.

Cover Credits: © AP Images (AIDS banner); NASA photo (Sally Ride); Ron Galella/WireImage/Ron Galella Collection/Getty Images (Michael Jackson); Science & Society Picture Library/SSPL/Getty Images (computer).

Contents

Introduction

Compared with the 1960s and 1970s, the decade of the 1980s was a very different time in the United States. During those two earlier decades, many Americans, especially the younger generation, had come to question the values that previous generations had taken for granted. The 1960s had been a time of heroic struggle for civil rights. It had also been a time of urban rioting and the assassinations of President John F. Kennedy, his brother Robert Kennedy, Dr. Martin Luther King Jr., and Malcolm X. The social upheavals in the 1960s brought about by the Vietnam War and opposition to it continued into the 1970s. Americans in the 1970s also witnessed the sorry spectacle of the Watergate scandal and President Richard Nixon's resignation from office. And the 1970s ended with the humiliating episode of Americans being held hostage in Iran.

By 1980, it was time for a change. Americans were tired of political protests. They were eager to feel good about themselves and their country again. Sensing their mood, Ronald Reagan campaigned for president on the theme of renewing good feelings about America. Thus began the 1980s.

The 1980s brought changes to everyday life. Personal computers, video games, and music videos were new. Electronics were changing the way people worked and played. Important changes also took place in world affairs. When the decade started, the United States and the Soviet Union were still bitter enemies. Their rivalry would shift in unexpected ways during the 1980s.

For decades, America and the Soviet Union had competed in the Cold War, a worldwide struggle for allies and resources. Both nations wielded great power. More than once, the Cold War nearly exploded into direct military conflict, and the threat of a nuclear war was always present. In 1980, the Winter Olympics became part of the Cold War rivalry when US and Soviet teams faced off for a hockey game later known as the Miracle on Ice.

America seemed to bounce back in the 1980s. The economy improved and unemployment fell. A space shuttle made its very first flight and proved that America was still a leader in technology. Yet the nation also experienced troubles during the decade. The virus HIV emerged, which caused tens of thousands of people to die from AIDS. Crack appeared on city streets and caused suffering and violence. In 1986, a space shuttle flight turned deadly and killed seven astronauts. A year later, the stock market crashed. Meanwhile, wars raged around the globe.

As the 1980s continued, the Cold War began to thaw. In 1985, the Soviet Union gained a new leader, Mikhail Gorbachev, who was unhappy with his country's condition. Gorbachev felt it was time to make changes. He wanted to overhaul the Soviet government and economy and improve relations with the United States. US President Ronald Reagan was a longtime critic of the Soviet Union. However, he welcomed Gorbachev's gestures of peace. For the first time in forty years, the end of the Cold War was in sight. In a single decade, the world had changed dramatically.

Gobachev (left) and Reagan sought peace between their countries.

Pop Culture, Lifestyles, and Fashion

America's economy steadily improved during the 1980s. This meant people had more money to spend. Suddenly, acquiring possessions and dressing to reflect one's success became important.

Consumer Spending

During the 1980s, shopping malls, which had first become popular in the suburban United States in the 1970s, continued to spread. Americans could now visit shopping malls in cities, as well as in small towns. Banks were eager to distribute credit cards to consumers. By the mid-1980s, the average credit-card holder carried seven cards. The easy credit, of course, resulted in an explosion of consumer debt. People flocked to stores and malls. In one six-year period during the mid-1980s, American consumers bought 62 million microwave ovens, 63 million VCRs, 57 million washers and dryers, 105 million color television sets, 31 million cordless phones, and 30 million telephone answering machines. During these same years, Americans also bought 88 million cars and light trucks.

Going to the mall became the favorite leisure-time activity of many Americans. But shopping did not stop at the mall. When they got home, Americans turned on their televisions. Two of the most

Shopping malls were a center of activity in the consumer-driven 1980s.

popular television channels were all about shopping—QVC and the Home Shopping Network. Now, people did not have to leave their homes to buy the products they wanted. They could call in and purchase items they saw on television, using their credit cards.

Yuppies

In order to keep on buying, Americans of the 1980s became more focused than ever on how to make money. Many of those who were in college or about to enter college planned to major in business. The MBA (Masters of Business Administration) degree was seen as the key to a successful career in corporate America. And the big corporations, which offered high starting salaries to new MBAs, were where young people wanted to work.

Young Americans building careers in business or in professions, such as medicine or law, became known as young urban professionals, or yuppies. The yuppie lifestyle involved total dedication to career and a willingness to work many hard hours in order to get ahead. The yuppie's goal was to have a successful career and the high standard of living made possible by that career. So many people were drawn to the yuppie lifestyle and yuppie values that *Newsweek* magazine decided to call 1984 the "Year of the Yuppie."

As more women entered the workplace, two-career families became common. Unlike during previous decades, many young married couples postponed having children until they had achieved financial security. The goal of making money replaced the ideals of social justice that had driven young people in the 1960s and 1970s. In 1985, Madonna released the song "Material Girl." It seemed to represent the desire of many Americans to acquire more and more things. The lyrics went, "We are living in a material world, and I am a material girl."

Culture of Greed

The 1987 movie *Wall Street* aptly portrayed the culture of greed that was prevalent in the 1980s. Michael Douglas *(left)* played the film's villain, a ruthless investor named Gordon Gekko. In one of cinema's most famous speeches, Gekko said, "Greed, for lack of a better word, is good." Although fictional, Gordon Gekko was based on real-life people known as corporate raiders who used their wealth to take over companies. Corporate raiders sought only to make money for themselves. Often their actions harmed the company and its workers.

At the time, greedy investors were viewed as smart businesspeople. However, it soon became clear that some of them were cheating. Stock trader Ivan Boesky pled guilty to fraud in 1986. Real estate investor Leona Helmsley was convicted of tax evasion in 1989. In 1990, bond investor Michael Milken was sentenced to ten years in prison for illegal trading. Their criminal acts showed the dangers of greed. Eventually, people lost respect for the corporate raiders and other selfish investors.

Power Dressing

The conservative, ambitious mood in the United States during the 1980s was reflected in styles of dress that were similar to those of the conservative 1950s. Yuppies wore dark-colored business suits to work, which came to be called power suits. A typical outfit for a professional working man of the 1980s consisted of a white dress shirt, silk tie, tailored jacket, and leather wing-tipped shoes. Men often slicked their hair back with gel. Women's clothing reflected their rising status in the business world. A woman would wear a below-knee-length skirt and a white blouse. A tailored jacket with shoulder pads helped project a powerful female image. It was important to yuppies that others recognize their success at first glance. Therefore, they wore expensive and noticeable items, such as Rolex watches. They also spent a lot of money so they could carry their cellular phones, first available in 1983, in fancy leather briefcases.

Preppy Becomes Trendy

The yuppies' leisure-time wardrobe also reflected 1950s styles, as well as a concern with status. Yuppies favored the preppy style—casual wear that gave the appearance of wealth. Items of clothing had visible labels on them so it would be clear that they were expensive. Typical clothes included classically styled jeans, khakis, or long shorts, shirts with conservative plaid prints or narrow stripes, white V-neck tennis sweaters, cable-knit sweaters, cotton turtlenecks, leather moccasins or penny loafers, Ralph Lauren shirts, and Calvin Klein underwear.

Working Out

Yuppies were great believers in physical fitness and were concerned about their appearance. They signed up for aerobic exercise classes in

health clubs to improve their bodies. Many believed that being physically fit would help them compete more effectively in the world of business. The fitness craze in the 1980s led to a new look in fashion. Various types of exercise gear began to be worn as everyday clothing. These new styles included one-piece bodysuits, stirrup pants, leg warmers, leggings, tights, tank tops, bicycle shorts, and jogging shorts. These items were often made of new snug-fitting fabrics, such as spandex.

Mohawks, Ripped Jeans, and Sweatsuits

While the yuppies were busy building their careers and trying to impress people with their clean-cut, affluent style of dress, other young Americans were heading in a different direction. Teen clothing styles during the 1980s reflected several different influences. The punk style, which had originated in England during the 1970s, featured black clothing, leather jackets, and ripped jeans. American punks, both male and female, wore earrings—sometimes several in one ear. They also pierced their noses and other body parts. They dyed their hair in bright colors. Some wore their hair in a style known as a Mohawk, in which most of the head was shaved to leave hair only down the middle of the scalp.

Another trend in teen fashion featured oversized clothes and clothes that looked old. Faded denim became popular, as did the practice of tearing shirts. This ragged, secondhand, low-cost look, known as grunge, was the opposite of the neat styles worn by yuppies. The grunge look first became popular in Seattle and then spread to the rest of the country. Another influence on teen fashion came from African American rap singers. In addition to oversized clothes, rappers wore brand-name sneakers without laces, baseball caps turned sideways or backward, and sweatsuits.

A Puzzling Cube

In every decade, certain fads quickly take the country by storm. Earlier decades saw such fads as the hula hoop and the pet rock. In 1980, Americans became obsessed with a puzzle known as the Rubik's Cube. Erno Rubik, a Hungarian professor of architecture, had invented his cube in 1974. He had first come up with the idea as a challenge for his students. Once a person tried to solve the puzzle, he or she often could not put it down. People became hooked on the cube and spent hours at a time trying to solve it. By the end of 1981, more than ten million Rubik's Cubes had been sold throughout the world.

The Rubik's Cube was a six-sided cube that consisted of twenty-six smaller cubes. The cubes could be rotated in any direction. The object was to end up with a different uniform color on each of the six sides of the Cube. There were more than forty-three quintillion (43,000,000,000,000,000,000) different positions possible for the smaller cubes. Of course, some people figured out how to do it. But many people could not, and it drove them crazy. As frustration mounted, a Cube Smasher became available. Advertisements said the Cube Smasher could beat the Rubik's Cube into forty-three quintillion pieces! More than one hundred thousand Cube Smashers were quickly sold.

Pac-Man

Another fad of the early 1980s was a video game called Pac-Man. Like the Rubik's Cube, Pac-Man had been invented during the 1970s. Namco Limited, the Japanese company that developed the game, based its name on the Japanese word *paku*, which means "to eat." The more dots Pac-Man devoured without being eaten by ghosts, the more points a player scored. Pac-Man appeared in video arcades in the United States in October 1980. Within eighteen months, Americans

Pop Culture's Influence on Fashion

More than ever, rock stars and TV shows influenced fashion. Teenage girls dressed like Madonna *(left)* by wearing black skirts with lace gloves and long necklaces. They teased up their hair with hairspray and added big bows. Young men copied the *Miami Vice* look. Stars of the TV police drama wore suit jackets over pastel T-shirts. They were unshaven and wore no socks with their shoes. The 1986 film *Top Gun*, which was about fighter pilots, made designer sunglasses trendy. The movie also added to the popularity of leather jackets. As the decade ended, rock music once again affected fashion. The ripped jeans and denim jackets worn by heavy-metal bands were in style.

HIGH SCORE
22400

Kids and teens spent hours in video arcades playing Pac-Man.

READY!

spent about $1 billion to rack up record scores. There were Pac-Man contests. Guidebooks, such as *How to Win at Pac-Man*, became best-sellers. Pac-Man soon became available in other formats, such as a computer cartridge game, board game, card game, and puzzle. There was even a Pac-Man wristwatch version that could be played anywhere.

Dolls of the Decade

The most memorable toy of the 1980s was a doll with fat cheeks and a pinched nose known as the Cabbage Patch Kid. Xavier Roberts, a young Georgia sculptor, created the first Cabbage Patch Kid. He had come up with the idea after discovering soft sculptures at arts and crafts fairs in the South. Coleco Industries, a toy company, agreed to mass produce Cabbage Patch Kids. Once these dolls appeared in toy stores in 1983, children all around the country fell in love with them. At first, many people thought the dolls were ugly. Kids loved them, however, and many soon regarded the dolls as adorable. Each Cabbage Patch Kid was unique in some way—some had dimples, pacifiers, or different hairstyles. Each doll came with "official" adoption papers. Cabbage Patch Kids became must-have items. Millions of the dolls were sold, and Coleco had trouble keeping up with the demand.

Entertainment and the Arts

Overall, the entertainment of the 1980s reflected the nation's new attitude of optimism and potential. Movies and music seemed bigger, more fun, and more expensive, and Americans had more money to spend on them.

Music That Soothed

In the 1980s, a new kind of music became popular, especially among yuppies. In general, this music, which came to be called New Age, tended to have a limited range of emotional expression. The music had a soothing effect on listeners and was great for relaxation and meditation. For those who needed a temporary escape from stress, New Age music was just the thing. The pleasant-sounding music, whether acoustic or electronic, featured repetitive melodies that did not seem to go anywhere. Pianist George Winston and harpist Andreas Vollenweider were among the most popular New Age musicians. Critics compared it to elevator Muzak. Some said that New Age music put them to sleep.

Alan Hunter was one of the original MTV VJs.

CDs Replace LPs

The compact disc, or CD, was first introduced in 1982. Suddenly, music fans were able to enjoy listening to their favorite music without hearing the scratches and other surface noises of vinyl records. The CD's crystal-clear sound quickly gained popularity. Some people insisted, however, that the CD sound was sterile. It lacked the warmth that they claimed they could detect on a vinyl LP. But most people preferred the CD. By the end of the 1980s, the LP was clearly on its way out. The CD was in.

I Want My MTV

Before the 1980s, music was mainly for the ears. Music lovers listened to records and the radio but had little to watch. That changed in 1981 with the arrival of Music Television, or MTV. The new channel played music videos twenty-four hours a day.

MTV was an instant hit with young people. For the first time, they could watch pop artists perform their latest hits. A video jockey, or VJ, introduced songs and talked about the performers. Early videos were simple and showed band members singing and playing instruments. Later, videos became more elaborate with narratives and special effects.

MTV was largely responsible for the growing popularity of music videos and new trends in music and dance. The 1980s saw the increasing popularity of break dancing, an acrobatic style of dance that involved spinning, touching parts of the body to the floor, and a tightly synchronized, almost robotic movement. The performers featured on MTV influenced the styles of music and dancing that were popular among young people. They also changed fashion, as teens copied the new trends seen in music videos.

Certain performers quickly realized the value of the music video. It enabled them to build a personal image that matched their music. Madonna and Michael Jackson were among the first artists to make use of MTV. Jackson's dazzling "Thriller" video debuted in 1983. Its huge popularity made Jackson a superstar. It also made MTV a driving force in the music industry. Today, there are many music video channels. The original MTV now devotes most of its airtime to full-length television shows.

Hip-Hop Gains Popularity

In the early 1980s, break dancing, along with rap music and graffiti, made up a cultural trend known as hip-hop. Break dancing had actually begun in the late 1970s among Hispanic and African American youths. It was often a kind of competition to see who could come up with the most amazing moves. Skilled break dancers seemed to defy gravity as they spun around quickly on their backs, shoulders, or heads.

Rap music was a form of poetry set to rhythm. It gave young African Americans an artistic means of expressing their outrage at the many injustices experienced by ghetto youth in their daily lives. Rap music, which started in the late 1970s in the South Bronx, became popular with both white and black young people in the 1980s. After years of resistance, MTV finally launched the daily program Yo! MTV Raps in the late 1980s, which was hosted by Fab Five Freddy. The show quickly became the most popular program on the network. Among the most famous rappers of the 80s were Afrika Bambaataa, Grandmaster Flash, Queen Latifah, Salt'n'Pepa, Tone-Loc, L. L. Cool J, and Ice T.

Members of the Rock Steady Crew break dance in New York City.

Graffiti: Vandalism or Art?

The various elements of hip-hop culture could all be seen as a form of protest. Graffiti had begun appearing on the walls of buildings and on subway cars and buses in the 1970s, which was a time of upheaval caused by the unpopular Vietnam War and the Watergate scandal, among other problems. Young people from urban ghettos who felt they had no chance to make it in the elite world of art galleries and museums saw graffiti as a way to make society aware of their existence. Many people considered graffiti a form of vandalism that messed up public spaces. But by the 1980s, graffiti art was beginning to be recognized by some critics as a serious form of artistic expression. Graffiti was even exhibited in art galleries. Among the most popular graffiti artists of the 1980s were Jean-Michel Basquiat, Keith Haring, and Fab Five Freddy.

The Music Stars of the 1980s

Many musical artists achieved fame and fortune in the 1980s. Some, such as Michael Jackson and Bruce Springsteen, had been performing and recording for a long time. But it was not until the 1980s that they became true superstars. In 1982, Michael Jackson released his album *Thriller,* which would eventually sell more than forty million copies. In the next few years, a Michaelmania craze swept the world. Millions of fans rushed out to buy items associated with Jackson's image. They bought Michael Jackson posters, notebooks, key chains, caps, and T-shirts. Jackson earned eight Grammy Awards for *Thriller.*

Bruce Springsteen, known as the Boss, hit the jackpot in 1984 with the release of his album *Born in the U.S.A.* Jackson and Springsteen benefited from the broadcasting of their videos on MTV.

Many other artists, such as Madonna, also used videos to build a huge following. Madonna had a shrewd strategy for promoting herself. She changed her image a number of times throughout the

Fab Five Freddy

Born Fred Brathwaite in 1960, Fab Five Freddy *(above, in front)* was an important player in New York City's arts scene in the 1980s. A talented graffiti artist, Freddy's connections and interests helped bridge the uptown hip-hop world with the downtown art world. This carried into music, as well. Freddy was a well-known rapper in New York, but he would become nationally known when his friend Debbie Harry dropped his name in her popular group Blondie's song "Rapture."

The song also introduced many rock and pop fans to rap. When MTV finally dedicated a show to rap, Fab Five Freddy would serve as host.

The epic music event
Live Nation *took place in*
London and Philadelphia.

1980s to generate excitement about what she was doing. Her songs and videos were a mix of dance numbers and romantic ballads.

The artist known as Prince became a superstar in 1984 with his album and movie *Purple Rain*. Other big music stars of the decade included Cyndi Lauper, Whitney Houston, Billy Joel, Pat Benatar, Lionel Richie, George Michael, and Bon Jovi. Superstars of previous decades, such as David Bowie, Rod Stewart, Phil Collins, Steve Winwood, Tina Turner, and Aretha Franklin, achieved new success in the 1980s. Popular groups of earlier years, such as the Rolling Stones and Grateful Dead, also continued to record and perform.

The Music Industry Helps Others

During the 1980s, many big names in the music business joined forces to raise funds for a variety of causes. In 1985, Michael Jackson and Lionel Richie wrote a song called "We Are the World." It was dedicated to raising money for famine relief in Ethiopia. In addition to an all-star chorus, the song featured solos by Jackson, Richie, Bruce Springsteen, Diana Ross, Bob Dylan, Ray Charles, Willie Nelson, Stevie Wonder, Paul Simon, Kenny Rogers, Tina Turner, Daryl Hall, Cyndi Lauper, and Huey Lewis. The song raised more than $50 million in 1985. The money was given to relief organizations to be distributed in Africa.

On July 13 of that same year, a musical event called Live Aid raised $70 million for Africa. The fourteen-hour-long concert took place simultaneously at two locations—Wembley Stadium in London and JFK Stadium in Philadelphia. The concert was broadcast live to 150 countries. The audience was estimated at 1.5 billion people. The top acts included Elton John, Mick Jagger, Tina Turner, Bob Dylan, Keith Richards, Madonna, Hall and Oates, George Michael, and Elvis Costello.

Another 1985 benefit concert called Farm Aid took place on September 22 in Champaign, Illinois. The purpose of this event was to make people aware of the problems faced by America's farmers. Organized by country singer Willie Nelson, it raised between $8 million and $9 million for the nation's farmers. Performers included country stars Johnny Cash, Waylon Jennings, and Loretta Lynn, as well as rock artists, such as Bob Dylan, Lou Reed, and Bon Jovi.

'80s Blockbusters

Almost all the biggest movie hits of the 1980s featured spectacular state-of-the-art computerized special effects. At the top of the list was *E.T. The Extra-Terrestrial* (1982). Directed by Steven Spielberg, the film told the story of a lonely young suburban boy (played by Henry Thomas) who became friends with an alien (E.T.) from another planet. The alien was a sweet, cuddly creature. Movie audiences young and old fell in love with him. *E.T.* eventually earned around $700 million at the box office worldwide.

Among the other top movies were other science-fiction fantasies, such as George Lucas's *The Empire Strikes Back* (1980) and *Return of the Jedi* (1983), both of which were sequels to his 1977 hit *Star Wars*. Lucas's Indiana Jones adventure films—*Raiders of the Lost Ark* (1981), *Indiana Jones and the Temple of Doom* (1984), and *Indiana Jones and the Last Crusade* (1989)—were all directed by Steven Spielberg. Also high on the list of 1980s hit movies were *Ghostbusters* (1984), *Back to the Future* (1985), *Top Gun* (1986), *Rain Man* (1988), and *Batman* (1989). Almost all of them were big-budget action-adventure or comedy films that appealed to Americans of the time, who were obsessed with better technology and flashy possessions.

Cable TV Changes the Game

A major change occurred in American television in the 1980s. Up until that decade, viewers could choose among three major networks—

John Lennon is Shot

On December 8, 1980, one question that had long been on the minds of music fans was settled for good. The Beatles would never again make music together.

That year, the life of one of the greatest stars in the history of music—John Lennon—came to a tragic end. Lennon was shot and killed outside his apartment in Manhattan by Mark David Chapman, a madman claiming to be a fan. Earlier that day, Lennon had signed an autograph for Chapman outside his apartment building. When he returned later that evening, the singer found Chapman waiting outside for him. Chapman fired five shots at Lennon, who was rushed to a nearby hospital but could not be saved.

Lennon's death shook music fans around the world. His wife, Yoko Ono, dedicated a nearby section of Central Park in his honor. Known as Strawberry Fields, the area has become a shrine to Lennon, as well as a place for park visitors to reflect and sing his songs.

Harrison Ford starred as Indiana Jones in Raiders of the Lost Ark.

NBC, CBS, and ABC—and several local stations. In the 1980s, cable television became available to a mass audience. Network broadcasting, which was supported by advertising dollars, was free to the viewer. But even though cable subscribers had to pay a monthly fee, cable television quickly grew in popularity. Suddenly, up to thirty channels were available. Americans appreciated the greater choice and variety in programming. Popular cable channels included MTV, VH-1, ESPN, HBO, Showtime, and TNT.

As cable television became more popular, the networks began to lose viewers. Because of competition from new cable channels, networks had to make changes in their traditional programming and scheduling. For example, in June 1980 Ted Turner began broadcasting news twenty-four hours a day on his Cable News Network (CNN). In response, the networks had to devote more programming time each day to news shows. In 1989, CNN broadcast a live round-the-clock report of the events unfolding in Tiananmen Square in Beijing. Americans watched in horror as Chinese troops crushed the pro-democracy demonstration. And they admired one brave young man who stood up before an oncoming tank.

Hit Shows of the 1980s

One of the most popular television shows during the 1980s was *The Oprah Winfrey Show*. Oprah Winfrey's daytime talk show was a huge success because of the deeply personal nature of the interviews she conducted. She and her guests discussed controversial topics that touched the lives of many viewers.

Popular sitcoms of the 1980s included *Cheers* and *The Cosby Show*. *Family Ties*, a popular comedy that reflected the times, featured ex-hippies whose kids embodied the materialism of the 1980s. Innovative dramas, such as *Hill Street Blues, L.A. Law*, and *St. Elsewhere*, expanded their storytelling into narratives that continued from week to week.

Nighttime soap operas were also popular in the 1980s. Piggybacking off the popularity of *Dallas*, which began in 1978, were shows such as *Dynasty, Falcon Crest,* and *Knots Landing.* Americans tuned in weekly to watch what their favorite characters—often the villains— were up to.

Against all odds, Team USA defeated the Soviets in the 1980 Olympics.

Sports

In the 1980s, America's favorite sports football, baseball, and basketball continued their popularity. The 1980s may have begun the era of the sports superstar. It was a time when professional athletes were paid more than ever and became a greater part of popular culture.

Miracle on Ice

The 1980 Winter Olympics were held in Lake Placid, New York. Ice hockey was among the most popular events, but Soviet teams had triumphed in the four previous Winter Olympics. Most hockey fans expected this Olympics to be no different.

The Soviet squad was packed with veterans of international competition. By contrast, the American team was made up of young college and minor-league players. In an exhibition game just a week before the start of the 1980 Olympics, the Soviet team had beaten the Americans by a score of 10–3.

On February 22, 1980, the teams faced off again with a chance at Olympic gold on the line. Today, American hockey fans remember the game fondly as the Miracle on Ice. The match was more than a simple hockey game. It became a symbol of the bitter Cold War rivalry between the United States and the Soviet Union.

The Soviet team took an early lead. However, the young Americans stayed strong and played hard. The huge crowd cheered them on with chants of "U-S-A!" About midway through the final period, the Americans scored to tie the game at 3–3. A couple minutes later, Team Captain Mike Eruzione fired a shot past the Soviet goaltender. The US team managed to hold on. As the game ended, the American players—and the crowd—erupted in celebration. The US team captured the gold medal. Their feat was a source of national pride.

Fans Endure a Baseball Strike

The American love affair with baseball continued throughout the 1980s, but it was put to a severe test during the 1981 season. Major league baseball players went on strike on June 12. The players and the team owners could not reach an agreement over salaries. The strike lasted until the end of July. The work stoppage caused the cancellation of 713 baseball games. Baseball players lost $30 million in wages, and team owners lost about $166 million in revenue.

The long strike not only led to bitter feelings between players and team owners but also made the fans angry. People who had always enjoyed either going to ball games or watching baseball on television became frustrated. Many wondered whether the fans would become so turned off that they might not return to watching baseball once the strike was settled. However, baseball survived. The fans did not desert their favorite teams. Indeed, by the end of the decade fifty million fans were attending major league games each year. And baseball revenues were more than $1 billion a year including television deals.

Olympic Boycott

Many people feel that international sports competition should have nothing to do with politics. Unfortunately, during the 1980s international politics often got in the way of sports.

Dodgers players stretch before their first post-strike game.

Martina Navratilova

During much of the 1980s, women's tennis was dominated by a player who is considered one of the sport's greatest—male or female. From 1982–1986, Martina Navratilova was ranked number one in women's singles and averaged a remarkable average of 96.8 percent wins. In 1983, she lost only one match. She was an accomplished doubles player, as well, and she is the only player in tennis history to hold the top spot in singles and doubles for more than two hundred weeks.

Navratilova was born in Czechoslovakia and sought political asylum in the United States in 1975. During this Cold War era, she was often painted by the media as a communist villain, particularly when she played America's sweetheart, Chris Evert. The two were and continue to be friends, and Evert admits she was much steelier than the sensitive Navratilova.

Navratilova was ranked in women's singles' Top 10 for twenty straight years! She was inducted into the International Tennis Hall of Fame in 2000.

In 1980, US President Jimmy Carter declared that the United States would not participate in the twenty-second Summer Olympic Games in Moscow. This action was taken to protest the Soviet Union's invasion of Afghanistan. Many American athletes were very bitter. They had worked very hard and trained for years to prepare themselves for the competition. Now some of them would never have the chance to compete in the Olympics.

Sixty-five other countries joined the United States in boycotting the Olympic Games in 1980. Four years later, the Soviet Union and its communist allies retaliated by boycotting the twenty-third Summer Olympic Games held in Los Angeles.

President Jimmy Carter announced that the United States would boycott the 1980 Summer Olympic Games in Moscow.

1984 Summer Olympics

The United States, among many other countries, had boycotted the 1980 Summer Olympics in Moscow for political reasons, which led many American athletes to sacrifice their Olympic dreams. Some of them would get another chance. In 1984 at the summer games held in Los Angeles, American Olympians won an astonishing 174 medals—more than three times the number won by the second-place team. Of those US medals, just fewer than half were gold.

The United States no doubt benefited from the boycotts of the Soviets and other Eastern Bloc nations, who traditionally excelled in gymnastics and weightlifting. One communist nation that ignored the boycott was Romania. That country would not let politics get in the way of sportsmanship, and they had a very good Olympics and placed second in the overall medal count.

San Francisco Earthquake Shakes Baseball

Perhaps one of the most memorable baseball events during the 1980s was a game that had to be postponed. On October 17, 1989, the San Francisco Giants and the Oakland Athletics were getting ready to play game three of the World Series at Candlestick Park in San Francisco. At exactly 5:04 P.M., about half an hour before game time, the San Francisco Bay Area was struck by a severe earthquake with a magnitude of 7.1 on the Richter scale. The entire stadium and the sixty-eight thousand fans in the stands were shaken by the rolling motion of the quake, which became known as the Loma Prieta earthquake.

Baseball fans all around the country were just sitting down to watch the game on television. They saw the ball players and their families rush out onto the field, where they would be safe. Fortunately, the fans were able to leave Candlestick Park safely, although there was some damage to the stadium. Other residents of the Bay Area were not so lucky. Buildings, freeways, and a section of the Oakland Bay Bridge collapsed. There were numerous fires. Sixty-three people were killed, and thousands were left homeless. Earthquake damage cost the area about $6 billion.

National and International Politics

On November 4, 1980, Americans elected Ronald Reagan to be their next president. Reagan would lead the country for most of the decade, and his presidency led to big changes in the country and around the globe.

A B-List Actor Is Elected President

Reagan defeated President Jimmy Carter in a landslide vote to become the fortieth president of the United States. It was clear that people wanted a change. They associated Carter with the failure to free United States citizens who were being held hostage in Iran. They also blamed him for economic problems caused, in part, by higher energy costs. Meanwhile, Reagan emphasized patriotism and promised prosperity.

Some people thought it odd that an actor, who had starred in many Hollywood B-list movies and hosted the television show *Death Valley Days*, had managed to become president of the United States. It was true that Reagan had gained political experience as governor of California. But how could an actor know how to lead the most powerful nation on earth? The fact is that acting skills can come in handy for a politician. Reagan was popular with the voters because he was

Ronald Reagan's administration defined the 1980s.

The hostages returned to the United States from captivity in Iran in 1981.

effective in getting his message across. Known as the Great Communicator, Reagan was even well liked by many who disagreed with his policies.

As president, Ronald Reagan helped America rise above the gloom of the 1970s. Reagan was nearly seventy years old when he took office. However, he showed an upbeat energy that people admired. Reagan wanted to make America strong again. He said that the government had grown too big, spent too much money, and hindered business. Reagan also called for a stronger military. Listeners found his words inspiring.

America still faced many challenges. The economy was struggling. One in every ten workers had no job. Food, gas, and other goods were expensive. Yet with Ronald Reagan leading the nation, people sensed that a change was taking place. America was bouncing back.

Iran Hostages Are Freed

On January 20, 1981, the day of Reagan's presidential inauguration and thereby Carter's last day in office, Iran released the fifty-two remaining American hostages who had been seized in Tehran at the US embassy. The hostages had been taken prisoner shortly after a revolution in Iran. The new Iranian government and its supporters held the embassy workers captive to blackmail the United States.

In April 1980, US special operations troops were sent to Iran on a secret mission to free the hostages. In the first part of the plan, eight helicopters and six large transport planes were supposed to land in a desert area southeast of Tehran. Later, after American soldiers had stormed the embassy compound and freed the hostages, helicopters would fly everyone out of Tehran.

Unfortunately, the helicopters flew into a heavy sandstorm as they approached the landing site in the desert. Three of the helicopters were damaged. With an inadequate number of aircraft, the mission was called off. As the aircraft were preparing to leave, one of the helicopters crashed into a transport plane and exploded, which killed eight US servicemen. The failure embarrassed the United States.

Iran released the hostages just minutes after Reagan was sworn in as president. They had spent 444 days in captivity. The nation celebrated their safe return.

President Reagan is Shot

On March 30, 1981, a gunman tried to kill President Ronald Reagan. The president was giving a speech at a hotel in Washington, D.C. Outside, a crowd gathered in hopes of catching a glimpse of Reagan as he walked to his waiting limousine. When the president emerged from the hotel, a man in the crowd pulled out a handgun and started firing. Reagan and three other people were hit.

Secret Service agents rushed the president to the hospital. Doctors treated his wounds. Within a month, Reagan was back at work in the White House. The ordeal made him even more popular with Americans. He had stayed upbeat even in the face of grave danger.

The gunman, John Hinckley Jr., was captured immediately after the shooting. Investigators learned that Hinckley was obsessed with actress Jodie Foster. He thought that shooting the president would impress her. John Hinckley was put on trial but found not guilty by reason of insanity. He was placed in a psychiatric hospital. He remains in custody today.

The other three shooting victims also survived, but one of them, presidential aide James Brady, was left partially paralyzed. Because of his experience, Brady supported gun control until his death in 2014.

President Reagan was shot by John Hinckley Jr. in 1981.

Jesse Jackson devoted himself to the underrepresented.

Reagan's Trickle-Down Economics

Ronald Reagan served two terms in office from 1981 to 1989. His economic policies tended to be conservative and favored the interests of big business and the wealthy. President Reagan believed that if taxes were lowered people—especially the wealthy—would have more spare funds and invest more money in corporations. If American businesses prospered as a result, they would create more jobs and give pay raises to their employees. This was seen as a trickle-down effect that would help poor people. So in 1981 and again in 1986, Reagan reduced rates for corporate and personal income taxes. Reaganomics, as this economic policy was called, was criticized by many as unfair to the poor. Many complained that the benefits never actually trickled down far enough to help lower-income people. However, Reaganomics was extremely popular among the yuppies and with businesspeople to whom it gave financial advantages.

Jesse Jackson's Rainbow Coalition

In 1984, Reverend Jesse Jackson campaigned to be the Democratic candidate for the presidency of the United States. He was the first African American to wage a full-scale campaign to head a major-party ticket. Jackson appealed to Americans who had not benefited from Reaganomics—African Americans, American Indians, Hispanics, and other minorities, as well as small farmers and poor Americans who had been adversely affected by cutbacks in government support and services. Jackson referred to those groups supporting him as the Rainbow Coalition. Jackson proposed a major public employment program, a renewal of federal spending on social services, expansion of civil rights, cutbacks in defense spending, and higher taxes for the rich.

For many years Jackson had fought long and hard for the expansion of civil rights for African Americans and other ethnic minorities. He became a well-known civil rights leader in the 1960s when he worked with Dr. Martin Luther King Jr. and his Southern Christian Leadership Conference. He continued his civil rights activism throughout the 1970s by forming Operation People United to Save Humanity, or PUSH, an organization devoted to inspiring African American high school students. In 1984, Walter Mondale won the Democratic candidacy for president but lost the election to Ronald Reagan. In 1988, Jackson waged another campaign in the Democratic primaries, but ultimately he finished second to Michael Dukakis, who then lost the election to George H.W. Bush, the father of future President George W. Bush.

The Homeless Crisis

During the 1980s, the sight of people living on the streets of America's cities became more common. Many people wondered how this could be happening in the world's richest nation. But it really was not a mystery. Throughout the decade, the cost of housing continued to rise. Among the street people were those who had jobs but could no longer afford to pay their rent or mortgage. There were also many who were incapable of working. Many people had become dependent on government support that was no longer available.

For these and other reasons, the number of homeless continued to rise. By the end of the decade, homelessness activists estimated that 2 million to 3 million Americans were living on the street, while the government's Department of Housing and Urban Development reported 250,000 to 300,000 homeless Americans. Whatever the exact figure, the numbers were growing.

Black Monday and the Stock Market Crash

President Reagan had promised to balance the budget. But his policies led to a dramatic growth in the federal deficit. In part, this was due

to his huge increase in spending for defense programs. It was partly due to lower tax revenues. Reagan's policies did lead to a lowering of the high inflation rates of the late 1970s and early 1980s. But by 1987, inflation was creeping up again, and interest rates were rising. During 1987, there was a wild burst of optimism in the financial markets. The stock market surged to record highs. But the upward movement could not last. During the late summer, stock prices headed lower. And on October 19, which came to be called Black Monday, the market fell 500 points, more than 20 percent. This was the biggest one-day drop since the stock market crash of 1929, which had set off the Great Depression. Luckily, the 1987 crash did not cause the same wide-spread panic and poverty as the Depression of the 1930s.

Wall Street workers headed home in shock on Black Monday, October 19, 1987, the day the stock market crashed more than 20 percent.

The War on Drugs Widens

In the 1980s, America experienced a surge in drug abuse when crack arrived on the scene. Crack was cheap, easy to obtain, and extremely addictive. Despite health dangers that include heart failure, liver damage, and death from overdose, the drug spread across the entire nation. The crack epidemic created many problems. Hospitals strained to treat an influx of overdose victims. Police struggled to contain a rise in crime. Rival drug dealers fought gun battles on city streets. Addicts robbed and stole so they could buy more crack.

President Reagan said that the nation needed to expand its war on drugs. Cities hired more police officers and created stricter laws targeted drug crimes. First Lady Nancy Reagan championed the Just Say No antidrug advertising campaign. Gradually, the crack epidemic began to decline. Still, abuse of illegal drugs would remain a major problem in the United States, and prisons would overcrowd as a result of Reagan's war on drugs.

Reagan's Strategic Defense Initiative

Ronald Reagan believed it was his patriotic duty to defeat communism. He referred to the Soviet Union as the "Evil Empire." Reagan poured hundreds of billions of dollars into a defense program known as the Strategic Defense Initiative, or SDI. The purpose of this program, which became known as Star Wars, was to develop a space-based system of weapons that could shield the United States from an attack by Soviet nuclear missiles. Critics of SDI said the program would never work. Unfortunately, they were right. The technology was never successfully developed, despite all the money that had been spent.

Korean Airlines Flight Shot Down

Although the Cold War between the United States and the Soviet Union would wind down toward the end of the decade, the two superpower rivals still regarded each other with hostility and suspicion in 1983. The Soviets were particularly sensitive to any violation of their airspace, especially after an incident in 1978 in which a Korean airliner had flown hundreds of miles over Soviet territory before it was shot at and forced to land. Soviet defense forces were authorized to stop any such intrusion by force. Unfortunately, on September 1, 1983, Korean Airlines flight 007 (KAL007) en route from the United States to Seoul, South Korea, strayed off course into Soviet airspace. After tracking the airliner, a Soviet fighter jet shot it down. All 269 passengers and crew members were killed. The incident seemed to validate President Ronald Reagan's characterization of the Soviet Union as an "Evil Empire," and Reagan referred to the tragedy as a "massacre."

Iran-Contra

President Reagan's desire to defeat communism wherever it might arise eventually got him into trouble. In 1981, he had directed the Central Intelligence Agency, or CIA, to help guerrilla forces in

George Keyworth served as Reagan's science advisor for Star Wars.

Lt. Col. Oliver North was blamed for the Iran-Contra affair.

Nicaragua overthrow Daniel Ortega's leftist Sandinista government.

In the fall of 1986, Congress learned that an illegal secret policy had been carried out by the Reagan administration to sell missiles to Iran in exchange for a release of United States hostages in the Middle East. The profits from the sale of arms were then used to fund operations of the guerrillas in Nicaragua, who were known as contras. These rebels were trying to overthrow the communist government of Nicaragua. Giving aid to the contras was against US law.

For a while, as Congress held televised hearings on the matter, it looked as if President Reagan might be impeached. However, others, including United States Marine Lieutenant Colonel Oliver North, were found to be responsible for the illegal activities. In 1989, North received a suspended three-year prison sentence and a $150,000 fine for his crimes. While no proof emerged that Reagan knew about the illegal funding of the contras, the Iran-Contra affair haunted Reagan for the rest of his time in office.

An End to the Cold War

Ronald Reagan's massive military buildup probably played a key role in the eventual end of the Cold War between the United States and the Soviet Union. The Soviet Union could not afford the huge costs of building and deploying new weapons systems. Indeed, although the United States did not know it at the time, the Soviet Union was growing steadily weaker through the 1980s. Several decades of mismanagement and corruption had taken their toll on the Soviet economy. When Mikhail Gorbachev came to power in 1985, he called for *perestroika*, or restructuring, of the Soviet economy. His goal was to decentralize economic decision making. He also called for a policy of *glasnost*, or openness, in which Soviet citizens would be entitled to freedom of speech and assembly.

Gorbachev also wanted to improve relations between the United States and the Soviet Union—the two superpowers. Over the next few years, he and Reagan met several times. Their long talks often got bogged down in complicated details. But the two leaders were finally able to negotiate sweeping new arms treaties, which called for a major reduction in the numbers of nuclear missiles on both sides.

In December 1988, Mikhail Gorbachev announced that the Soviet Union was withdrawing many of its weapons from Eastern Europe. Shortly after, the communist governments of the Eastern European countries all fell. For years, communist East Germany had kept people from leaving or entering the nation by force. The Berlin Wall was the most famous symbol of the closed communist state. On November 9, 1989, East Germany opened its borders. The next day, East and West Germans together began tearing down the Berlin Wall, which had divided the city of Berlin since August 1961. Although many people around the world could hardly believe it, the Cold War finally seemed to be coming to an end.

The Tiananmen Square Massacre

The 1980s were a fateful time for other communist nations, as well. While Soviet leader Mikhail Gorbachev had begun allowing more freedoms in the Soviet Union in response to his citizens' wishes, things were different in China. When Chinese citizens demanded change, their government said no. In 1989, China's Army killed hundreds of protestors in an incident known today as the Tiananmen Square massacre.

China's communist government strictly controlled the lives of its people. They had little freedom. Because the government controlled the economy, most people were impoverished. In the 1980s, China began making small changes to its communist system. The government gave

Mikhail Gorbachev wanted to improve relations with the US.

Pro-democracy demonstrators filled Tiananmen Square.

up a little bit of its control over the economy and began experimenting with free elections at the local level. Chinese people liked the reforms and wanted more. College students were especially vocal about further changes.

In April 1989 a group of students gathered at Tiananmen Square in the Chinese capital of Beijing to mourn the passing of reform hero Hu Yaobang. In the days that followed, they were joined by more students and Chinese workers. The large crowd began demanding an end to communism in China. The nation's communist leaders refused. Protests at Tiananmen Square grew larger and louder. By May, more than one hundred thousand students and workers were marching on the square each day. Protests had also sprung up in other Chinese cities.

By early June, China's communist leaders decided to end the protests. They sent the Army to clear Tiananmen Square. Tanks and at least ten thousand soldiers surrounded the square on June 3 and ordered the students to disperse. On the morning of June 4, according to Western eyewitnesses, the students filed out of Tiananmen Square peacefully. But soon afterward, Chinese soldiers began firing at students and residents of Beijing who supported them. The violence continued for several days. Hundreds of people were killed. Thousands more were injured.

For months, the Chinese government continued its crackdown. Many protestors were tracked down and arrested. Some were executed. Chinese officials banned foreign news reporters. The progress gained from China's reforms was lost. Many nations condemned the Tiananmen Square massacre. In China, it remains a forbidden subject even today.

Deadly Conflicts Around the World

During the 1980s, limited—if often very brutal—wars raged all around the globe. In September 1978, there was good reason to be hopeful that there would finally be peace in the Middle East. Egyptian

President Anwar Sadat and Israeli Prime Minister Menachem Begin, with the help of United States President Jimmy Carter, had negotiated a peace agreement called the Camp David Accords. The agreement was signed in 1979. But in 1981, Sadat was assassinated by fanatics who considered him a traitor for holding peace talks with Israel. In the Middle East, trying to make peace proved to be a dangerous business.

In 1980, Iraq attacked its neighbor Iran in a border dispute. The resulting war lasted throughout most of the decade. Thousands of people lost their lives.

Meanwhile, farther to the east in Afghanistan, the United States gave money and arms to guerrillas called *mujahideen,* or holy warriors, who were battling the Soviet Army. Finally, in 1989, the Soviets withdrew from Afghanistan. The United States would later be haunted by their involvement in this conflict.

The civil war that began to rage in Lebanon during the 1970s continued through most of the 1980s. Yasser Arafat's Palestine Liberation Organization, or PLO, which had been struggling for years to create a separate state for Palestinian people, attacked northern Israel from bases in Lebanon. In 1982, the Israeli Army invaded Lebanon in an attempt to destroy PLO bases. When the Israelis reached Beirut, the United States helped arrange a plan to allow the PLO to leave. United States Marines were sent to help evacuate PLO fighters.

On April 18, 1983, the United States Embassy in Beirut was blown up. Sixty-three people were killed. Then on October 23, 1983, 241 United States Marines were killed when the United States Marine headquarters in Lebanon was blown up. The explosions killed 241 American servicemen and 58 French soldiers. In 1984, United States peacekeeping forces were withdrawn from Lebanon. The civil war continued.

US-armed mujahideen fought the Soviet army in the Afghan mountains.

A US Marine guards the Beirut embassy after it was bombed.

In 1982, Britain and Argentina fought a ten-week conflict called the Falklands War over islands in the South Atlantic Ocean that both countries claimed to own. In April, Argentine troops invaded the islands. Britain sent an armada of warships in response. After many fierce battles in which more than nine hundred soldiers and sailors were killed, Argentina surrendered in June. Nevertheless, the underlying cause of the war was never resolved. Today, both countries still claim ownership of the Falkland Islands.

In 1979, the government of the tiny Caribbean nation Grenada was overthrown. The new prime minister, Maurice Bishop, forged friendly relations with the Soviet Union and Cuba, which did not please American officials. President Ronald Reagan accused Cuba of planning to use Grenada as a base for spreading communist revolutions in Central America. In October 1983, Bishop was overthrown and killed by a group of army officers and an openly communist military government took power. President Reagan quickly ordered an invasion of Grenada and claimed that American students at a medical school there were in danger. On October 25, the first US invasion troops landed. Grenadian soldiers, as well as several hundred Cubans on the island, fought fiercely. But within a few days, American forces had defeated most of them and toppled the military government.

Women in Charge

Margaret Thatcher, who had become the Conservative party's prime minister of Great Britain in 1979, led her country throughout the 1980s. Not only was she the first female British prime minister, but she became the first British prime minister to be elected three times. Known as the Iron Lady, she was a forceful leader who never hesitated to fight for what she believed in. When Argentina invaded the Falkland Islands in 1982, Thatcher sent naval forces to retake British territory. After a three-week-long war, the Argentine forces surrendered.

In 1986, Corazon Aquino became president of the Philippines when she defeated President Ferdinand Marcos in an election. Her husband, Benigno Aquino, who was assassinated at Manila Airport in 1983, had been a political opponent of Marcos's. Marcos tried to steal the election from Corazon Aquino. But the people were outraged. Millions took to the streets to protest. Marcos and his wife, Imelda, were forced to flee the Philippines.

When Benazir Bhutto became prime minister of Pakistan in 1988, she became the first female leader of a Muslim nation. Her father, Zulfikar Ali Bhutto, a former prime minister of Pakistan, had been overthrown in 1977 by General Mohammad Zia ul-Haq, who sent Ali Bhutto to jail and later had him hanged. Benazir and her mother had to spend time in jail while Zia ruled the country. In 1988, Zia was killed in a plane crash. Benazir Bhutto then succeeded the same man who had ousted her father.

In the United States in 1981, President Ronald Reagan appointed Sandra Day O'Connor as an associate justice to the United States Supreme Court. She became the first female Supreme Court justice in United States history.

US Troops Invade Panama

In 1988, Americans elected George Herbert Walker Bush to be their next president after he had served for eight years as vice president in the Reagan administration. His son, George W. Bush, would later serve as president for two terms between 2000 and 2008.

In December 1989, the elder Bush ordered a United States invasion of Panama. Bush and his advisors had decided that it was necessary to remove General Manuel Noriega, Panama's leader, from power. When Manuel Noriega first rose to power in 1983, America had supported him. However, his actions quickly proved alarming. Noriega rigged elections and used violence to silence his opponents.

Salman Rushdie Is Forced Into Hiding

In February 1989, the Ayatollah Ruholla Khomeini, the spiritual and political leader of Iran, issued a *fatwa*, or death sentence, for a writer by the name of Salman Rushdie. Rushdie had written *The Satanic Verses*, a novel in which he dared to make fun of the Islamic religion. Muslims around the world were outraged by the novel, and many supported the death sentence. Riots broke out in cities in India and Pakistan. Muslims in London, where Rushdie was living, threatened to kill him on sight. Rushdie was forced to go into hiding. He remained out of public sight for years until the *fatwa* was finally lifted in September 1998.

US troops patrol the Vatican embassy where Noriega was hiding.

Although Noriega had been working for the United States Army and the CIA from 1955 to 1986, he had been caught selling United States secrets to communist Cuba and the Soviet Union. In 1988, Noriega was indicted by the United States on drug trafficking charges. US President George H. W. Bush tried to force the Panamanian dictator to resign. When that failed, Bush ordered an invasion of Panama. During the 1989 invasion, Noriega was captured and brought to the United States. He would eventually be tried, convicted, and sent to prison.

Advances in Science, Technology, and Medicine

The 1980s saw many triumphs and tragedies in the world of science. Artificial hearts and diagnostic imaging extended lives while nuclear, environmental, and natural disasters wreaked havoc on earth.

Rise of the Computer

The first electronic computer was invented in the 1940s. It was the size of a building and worked very slowly. By the 1970s, computers were smaller and faster. However, they were still expensive. Only businesses could afford them. In the 1980s, computers became less costly. For the first time, a family could buy one for the home. The age of personal computers, or PCs, had arrived.

Various companies developed home computers. Two eventually came to dominate the market: Apple and IBM. Two young men started Apple in a family garage. With clever ideas, they built their tiny business into a huge corporation. IBM, their rival, was already a huge corporation. For decades, IBM had pioneered the computer industry. Meanwhile, a small company called Microsoft began making programs for their computers. Microsoft quickly became the world leader in software.

The Apple III personal computer was introduced in 1980.

At first, people bought computers mainly to play games, such as Pac-Man. Eventually, with the development and availability of new software, word processing and spreadsheets became the most popular kinds of computer software. By today's standards, computers of the 1980s were primitive. They had blocky graphics and little memory, and they were not connected to the World Wide Web. Still, the computer age was beginning.

The Scourge of AIDS

AIDS, or acquired immunodeficiency syndrome, was first identified in 1981. The deadly disease would go on to become a global epidemic.

In 1984, researchers discovered that AIDS is caused by HIV, or human immunodeficiency virus. The virus makes a person's body unable to protect itself from other diseases. As a result, AIDS patients may

During the 1983 Gay Parade in New York City, a group holds a banner advocating the need for more AIDS research and empathy towad those affected by the deadly disease. Because not much was known about AIDS, people suffering from it ofen faced discrimination.

Ryan White

Ryan White was a boy from Indiana who suffered from hemophilia, a disease that prevents blood from clotting properly. He contracted HIV from a tainted blood transfusion. In 1984, thirteen-year-old Ryan was diagnosed with AIDS and was given six months to live.

When Ryan's condition became known around his hometown, many parents and teachers tried to keep him from attending school. At the time, most people did not understand AIDS. They thought a person could get the disease simply by being around someone who had it.

The fight for Ryan's right to attend school became news around the country. Because of his young age and his grace under terrible circumstances, he became a symbol of the AIDS epidemic. Ryan White died in 1990 at age eighteen. He outlived his doctor's prediction by five years.

suffer from many illnesses. A person can get the virus by having unprotected sex with an infected partner or by coming into contact with infected blood—for example, through the sharing of a hypodermic needle. An infected mother may unknowingly pass the virus on to her baby, as well.

During the 1980s, AIDS was a major concern in the United States. By the end of the decade, hundreds of thousands of Americans were infected with AIDS. Once people learned the proper precautions, however, the number of AIDS cases declined. Even so, an estimated fifty-six thousand Americans still contract the virus each year. In other parts of the world, the infection rate is much higher. Scienti have yet to find a cure for AIDS. However, new drugs are helpi AIDS victims live longer.

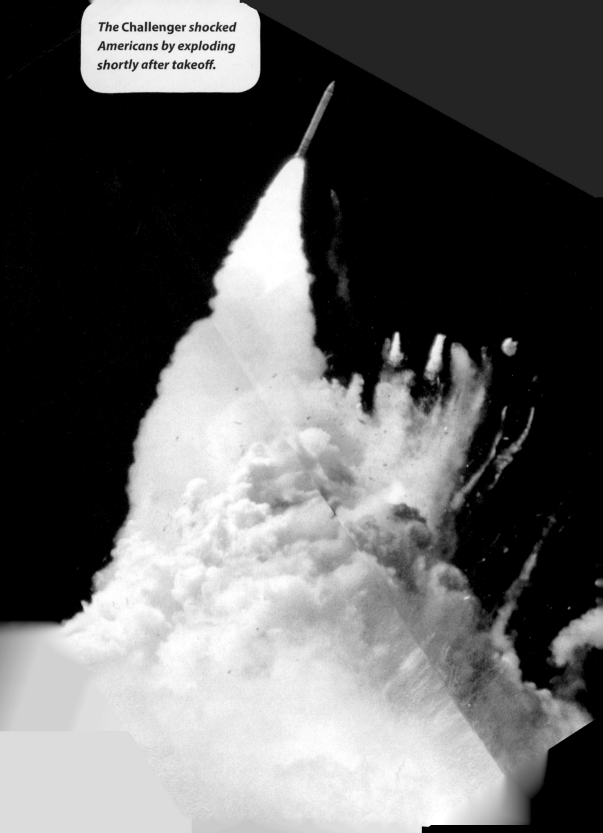

The Challenger *shocked Americans by exploding shortly after takeoff.*

Space Shuttles

In 1981, America launched the world's first space shuttle. Unlike other spacecraft, the space shuttle could fly back to earth like an airplane. Thus, it was reusable and could go on many missions. The space shuttle was the one of the most complex machines ever built. It could carry huge objects into orbit. It supported life for up to seven astronauts, who could conduct experiments in space, fix broken satellites, and perform other missions.

The first working space shuttle, *Columbia*, blasted off for its first mission on April 12, 1981. Anxious crowds cheered as the ship's powerful rocket boosters sent it into space. It was a proud moment for America. Eventually, NASA would add four more space shuttles to its fleet: *Challenger*, *Discovery*, *Atlantis*, and *Endeavour*.

Two of the shuttles would be stricken by tragedy. On January 28, 1986, millions of school children across America were watching a special television broadcast at their schools. Millions of other Americans were also watching. Christa McAuliffe, a high-school social studies teacher from New Hampshire, was about to make history as the first ordinary citizen to travel into space. She was part of the crew of astronauts aboard the space shuttle *Challenger*.

There was excitement in the air as the *Challenger* blasted off. But about seventy-four seconds later, excitement turned to shock and grief. The *Challenger* exploded, and everyone on board was killed. The tragedy served as a reminder that space travel is still extremely dangerous, and all who venture into space are true heroes. An investigation pointed to a faulty seal on one of the shuttle's rocket engines as the cause of the explosion. The shuttle astronauts had no chance at survival. NASA did not launch another space shuttle for more than two years.

In 2003, *Columbia* was lost during an accident. This tragedy, too, claimed the lives of all astronauts aboard. The remaining three shuttles were retired in 2011.

Improvements on the X-Ray

Magnetic resonance imaging (MRI) and nuclear magnetic resonance (NMR) were new ways of viewing the inside a person's body. The patient is placed in the field of an electromagnet and then subjected to radio waves. The images produced give doctors much better information than X-rays. MRI and NMR are used in the diagnosis of brain tumors, spinal disorders, multiple sclerosis, and heart disease. Unfortunately, the new technology, when first introduced, was very expensive. Only large hospitals could afford it. By the 1990s, it would be cheaper and much more commonly used.

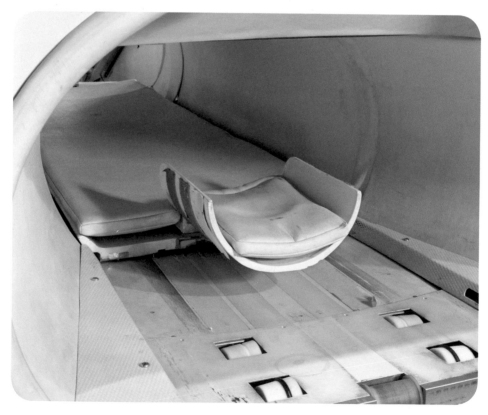

Introduced in the 1980s, magnetic resonance imaging (MRI) was a vast improvement over the X-ray.

The Jarvik-7

In 1982, Dr. Barney Clark became the first person to receive an artificial heart to replace his own diseased heart permanently. Clark lived for 112 days after the device, known as the Jarvik-7, was implanted. William Schroeder, who also received a Jarvik-7, lived for 620 days. This was an amazing medical breakthrough to be sure, but there were problems with it. The patient had to be hooked up to air compressors outside the body. And there was a constant danger of blood clots forming in the Jarvik-7. Eventually, doctors realized that the device could only be used as a temporary measure until a real heart was put in the patient. But there was hope that one day a self-contained artificial heart could be implanted that would allow the patient to live a normal life.

The Chernobyl Nuclear Disaster

On April 26, 1986, an explosion took place at a nuclear power station in Chernobyl, Ukraine, which was then part of the Soviet Union. The explosion ripped apart the nuclear reactor. Radioactive material scattered over an area of 32,000 square miles. More than 30 people died in the explosion and fire. About 133,000 people in the surrounding area had to be evacuated. Belarus, just north of Ukraine, received a heavy dose of radiation. Radioactive fallout from the explosion also affected many other parts of northern and western Europe. The final death toll from the disaster may reach as high as 30,000 to 40,000 people in the coming years as people develop cancer and other illnesses due to radiation exposure.

The Chernobyl disaster sent shock waves around the world. People wondered if the nuclear reactors in their own countries were safe. The antinuclear movement gathered steam. Although Americans had already experienced their own nuclear crisis with the Three Mile Island incident in 1979, more people in the US and in other countries began to call for an end to construction of new nuclear plants after Chernobyl. They also pressed for those nuclear plants that had a history of problems and seemed to be particularly dangerous to be shut down.

As it happened, plans for building new nuclear power plants in the United States had already been put on hold for a different reason. It was getting too expensive to build and maintain nuclear power plants. Other ways of generating electricity, such as burning fossil fuels including coal and oil, had become much cheaper.

The Chernobyl disaster showed that nuclear energy requires extreme caution. Since then, nuclear power plants have become safer. Engineers learned from the mistakes made at Chernobyl. Today, nuclear power plants create roughly 15 percent of the world's electricity.

Union Carbide Disaster

The American-owned Union Carbide insecticide plant in Bhopal, India, was a disaster waiting to happen. And on December 3, 1984, it happened. There was a leak of toxic gas at the plant. As a result, an estimated 3,500 to 6,400 people died, and 50,000 to 300,000 were seriously injured. Naturally, local residents were outraged.

The disaster pointed out the terrible mistake of building industrial plants in the midst of heavily populated residential areas. In 1989, the government of India sued Union Carbide. The company agreed to pay the victims of the disaster and their families $470 million in damages.

The Chernobyl disaster was another nail in the coffin of nuclear power.

Mount St. Helens

One of the worst natural disasters of the 1980s was the eruption of Mount St. Helens. The volcano in southwestern Washington, near the Oregon border, had been quiet for more than one hundred years. Then on May 18, 1980, at 8:32 A.M., it awakened with a mighty roar. Pressure had been building inside the volcano for almost two months, as indicated by the venting of smoke and ash. Then an earthquake caused a massive landslide of rock, ice, and snow on the mountain.

The pressure in the volcano was released in a huge eruption as powerful as the explosion of five hundred Hiroshima-sized atomic bombs according to one scientist. The eruption blasted away the top 1,313 feet of Mount St. Helens, which is about 8.8 billion cubic yards of mass. The massive plume of ash from the eruption rose sixteen miles into the sky. The blast of heated gas flattened forests for up to fifteen miles. Rivers became raging torrents of mud and washed away bridges and homes. Some towns in eastern Washington were coated with up to seven inches of volcanic ash. Fifty-seven people died as a result of the eruption. By the evening of May 18, Mount St. Helens was a smoking crater. What had been a 9,677-foot-tall mountain was now only 8,364 feet high. The Mount St. Helens National Volcanic Monument was created in 1982 and has become a major tourist attraction.

The Exxon *Valdez* Disaster

On March 24, 1989, the oil tanker Exxon *Valdez* was sailing southward in Alaska's Prince William Sound. The huge ship was carrying a full load of oil when it ran aground on a reef. The result was one of the worst environmental disasters in American history. 240,000 barrels of crude oil, which is approximately 11 million gallons, spilled into the waters of the Sound.

The accident was a catastrophe for the environment of Prince William Sound. Untold numbers of fish, birds, and mammals died. The fishing industry of the local villages was wiped out. Beaches along hundreds of miles of seacoast were coated in oil.

The Exxon *Valdez* oil spill had a devastating impact on wildlife. Many populations were still affected twenty-five years later.

Conclusion

The 1980s are remembered as a decade of extravagance and greed. After the troubles of the 1960s and 1970s, Americans were relieved to live in relative prosperity. There were plenty of new fads and gadgets to spend money on. The decade also was marked by remarkable discoveries and achievements in science and technology, not to mention political achievements, such as the end of the decades-long Cold War. However, the 1980s also brought such tragedies as the *Challenger* disaster, the Exxon *Valdez* oil spill, Chernobyl, and AIDS to the attention of Americans and the whole world. Perhaps best remembered for unique music, fashions, and outrageous celebrity personalities, the 1980s were a time of triumph and tragedy—a time that is sure to continue to have an impact for many years to come.

As the 1980s came to a close, a huge shift in global affairs was underway. The Soviet Union was collapsing, and Moscow's grip on the countries of Eastern Europe had loosened. In those countries, people were demanding more freedom, democracy, and an end to communism. By the early 1990s, Eastern Europe's communist regimes would all be replaced and the Soviet Union itself would no longer exist. With the Cold War over, many people hoped that a new era of peace and democracy would begin.

Unfortunately, new conflicts would erupt in the 1990s. In some cases, the roots of these wars lay in events of the previous decade. Yugoslavia, a country in southeastern Europe made up of many ethnic groups, had been held together in part by the threat of a Soviet takeover. With the collapse of the Soviet Union, that threat no longer

Michael Jackson revolutionized pop music in the 1980s.

existed. In the early 1990s, simmering ethnic resentments in Yugoslavia exploded into civil war.

Iraq's long war with Iran during the 1980s left it deep in debt to other Arab countries, including Kuwait and Saudi Arabia. Iraqi dictator Saddam Hussein wanted his war debts forgiven. When the Arab countries refused, Saddam ordered an invasion of Kuwait. American troops were rushed to Saudi Arabia to protect that country from further Iraqi aggression. Later, in the Gulf War, a US-led international force defeated Iraq and liberated Kuwait. But Saddam remained in power, and American troops remained in Saudi Arabia. Both situations would cause trouble for America throughout the 1990s and beyond.

Other trends in the 1990s were more positive. The number of AIDS sufferers would decrease, although a cure would not be discovered. Arts and entertainment would turn from frivolity to substance. Personal computers became more and more powerful. Increasing numbers of people bought PCs. And the rise of the Internet made possible new ways of learning, sharing information, and doing business.

Timeline

1980   Ronald Reagan is elected United States president. Rubik's Cube first hits the market. Pac-Man is first introduced. John Lennon is murdered by Mark Chapman. CNN begins broadcasting. The United States boycotts the Summer Olympic Games to protest the Soviet Union's invasion of Afghanistan. War begins between Iran and Iraq.

1981   MTV premieres. Hostages held in Iran are freed. Ronald Reagan is shot in an assassination attempt. Major-league baseball players go on strike. Reagan appoints Sandra Day O'Connor as the first female United States Supreme Court justice. AIDS is first identified. Reagan orders the CIA to overthrow Daniel Ortega's government in Nicaragua. Egyptian President Anwar Sadat is assassinated.

1982   Compact discs (CDs) are introduced. *E.T. The Extra-Terrestrial* premieres in theaters. Barney Clark receives the first permanent artificial heart. Michael Jackson releases his *Thriller* album.

1983   Cellular phones become available. Cabbage Patch Kids appear in toy stores and cause a frenzy among children and parents. The United States Embassy in Beirut is blown up.

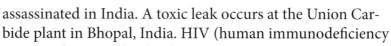

1984   *Newsweek* announces the "Year of the Yuppie." Bruce Springsteen releases his *Born in the U.S.A.* album. Prince releases *Purple Rain*. The Soviet Union and other communist countries boycott the Summer Olympics. United States forces leave Lebanon. Indira Gandhi is assassinated in India. A toxic leak occurs at the Union Carbide plant in Bhopal, India. HIV (human immunodeficiency virus) is discovered to be the cause of AIDS.

1985   Madonna releases "Material Girl," which echoes the materialistic sentiments of Americans. "We Are the World" debuts to raise money to end famine in Africa. Live Aid concerts are held to help African famine victims. A Farm Aid concert is held to benefit American farmers. Mikhail Gorbachev comes to power in the Soviet Union and institutes reforms.

1986 The space shuttle *Challenger* explodes on January 28. Congress learns of the Iran-Contra scandal. Corazon Aquino is elected president of the Philippines. The nuclear power station at Chernobyl in the Soviet Union has a serious explosion.

1987 The stock market crashes on October 19. President Reagan makes a speech in West Berlin imploring the Soviet Union to "tear down this wall!" *Wall Street*, a movie that depicts the decade's culture of corporate greed, is released.

1988 The Soviet Union announces the withdrawal of weapons from Eastern Europe. Benazir Bhutto becomes prime minister of Pakistan. George Herbert Walker Bush is elected United States president.

1989 The Tiananmen Square uprising takes place in Beijing, China. The San Francisco earthquake devastates parts of California. Oliver North receives a three-year suspended sentence for his role in the Iran-Contra scandal. The Berlin Wall is torn down in November, symbolizing the end of the Cold War. Ayatollah Khomeini issues a death sentence against Salman Rushdie, author of *The Satanic Verses*. President Bush orders the invasion of Panama to remove Manuel Noriega from power. The Exxon *Valdez* oil spill devastates Alaska's Prince William Sound.

Glossary

activist—A person who works to advance an idea or cause.

AIDS—A disease that weakens the body's ability to fight off other diseases.

boycott—To abstain or withdraw from relations with a person, organization, or event in protest.

Cold War—A struggle for global dominance between the United States and the Soviet Union that lasted from the late 1940s until 1991.

communism—A type of government in which all citizens are supposed to work for the good of society and share property equally.

corporation—A business or other organization that exists as its own legal entity.

crack—A solid form of cocaine that is smoked.

epidemic—The outbreak of an infectious disease.

fatwa—An Islamic legal pronouncement or decree.

guerilla—Rebel member of an independent group of soldiers fighting the group in authority that use irregular or impromptu tactics.

indict—To formally charge with a crime.

mujahideen—Radical guerilla soldiers fighting in the name of Islam.

nuclear—Relating to energy that comes from the splitting or merging of atoms.

superpower—An extremely powerful country, especially one that leads other countries.

trafficking—The trading or transporting of an illegal substance.

yuppie—A young urban professional who works in a city, makes a substantial living, and enjoys fine things.

Further Reading

Books

Berlatsky, Noah. *The Exxon Valdez Oil Spill*. Detroit, Mich.: Greenhaven Press, 2011.

Boshier, Rosa. *Ronald Reagan*. Minneapolis, Minn.: Essential Library, 2013.

Lusted, Marcia Amidon. *The Chernobyl Disaster*. Minneapolis, Minn.: Essential Library, 2011.

Sirota, David. *Back to Our Future: How the 1980s Explain the World We Live in Now*. New York, N.Y.: Ballantine Books, 2011.

Sonenklar, Carol. *AIDS*. Minneapolis, Minn.: Twenty First Century Books, 2011.

Zuchora-Walske, Christine. *The Berlin Wall*. Minneapolis, Minn.: Abdo Publishing Company, 2014.

Web Sites

inthe80s.com/index.shtml
This Web site celebrates the 1980s.

80s.com/
The '80s Server is fun site with games and entertainment dedicated to the decade.

whitehouse.gov/history/presidents/rr40.html
The official White House fact page for Ronald Reagan.

Movies

Wall Street. Directed by Oliver Stone. Los Angeles, Calif.: 20th Century Fox, 1987.

In this iconic movie, 1980s greed is in full-force.

Miracle. Directed by Gavin O'Connor. Burbank, Calif.: Walt Disney Pictures, 2004.

This movie dramatizes Team USA's remarkable victory in the 1980 Olympics.

Index

graffiti, 24, 26, 27
Grenada, 67
grunge look, 15

H

Haring, Keith, 26
Hinckley, John W. Jr., 48
homelessness, 52
home shopping, 11
human immunodeficiency virus
  (HIV), 7, 74, 75

I

India, 69, 80
Iran, 44, 47, 48, 64, 69, 86
Iran-Contra scandal, 56, 59

J

Jackson, Michael, 24, 26, 29
Jackson, Reverend Jesse, 51, 52
Jarvik-7, 79
Just Say No, 55

K

Khomeini, Ayatollah Ruholla, 69
Korean Airlines flight 007
  (KAL007), 56

L

Lebanon, 64
Lennon, John, 31
Live Aid, 29
Loma Prieta earthquake, 43

M

Madonna, 11, 17, 24, 26, 29
magnetic resonance imaging
  (MRI), 78
Marcos, Ferdinand, 68
McAuliffe, Christa, 77
Mondale, Walter, 52
Mount St. Helens, 82
MTV (Music Television), 23, 24,
  26, 27, 33
mujahideen, 64

N

Navratilova, Martina, 40
New Age music, 20
Nicaragua, 59
Noriega, Manuel, 68, 71
North, Oliver, 59

O

O'Connor, Sandra Day, 68
Olympics, 7, 37, 41, 42
Ono, Yoko, 31
Operation PUSH (People United
  to Save Humanity), 52
Ortega, Daniel, 59

P

Pac-Man, 16, 19, 74
Pakistan, 68, 69
Palestine Liberation Organization
  (PLO), 64
Panama, 68, 71
perestroika, 59
personal computer (PC), 6, 72, 86
Philippines, 68

physical fitness, 13, 15
preppy style, 13
Prince, 29
Prince William Sound, 82, 83
punk, 15

R

Rainbow Coalition, 51
rap music, 24, 27
Reaganomics, 51
Reagan, Ronald, 6, 44, 47, 48, 51,
  52, 55, 56, 59, 60, 67, 68
Roberts, Xavier, 19
Rubik, Erno, 16
Rubik's Cube, 16
Rushdie, Salman, 69

S

Sadat, Anwar, 64
Sandinistas, 59
San Francisco, California, 43
Satanic Verses, The, 69
shopping malls, 9
soap operas, 34
Soviet Union, 6, 7, 37, 38, 41, 42,
  56, 59, 60, 64, 67, 71, 79, 84
Spielberg, Steven, 30
Springsteen, Bruce, 26, 29
Star Wars. *See* Strategic Defense
  Initiative (SDI).
stock market crash, 7, 54
Strategic Defense Initiative (SDI),
  56

T

Thatcher, Margaret, 67
Tiananmen Square, 33, 60, 63
Turner, Ted, 33

U

Union Carbide disaster, 80

V

Vollenweider, Andreas, 20

W

Wall Street, 12
"We Are the World," 29
Winfrey, Oprah, 33
Winston, George, 20
World Series, 43

Y

yuppies, 11, 13, 15, 51